FUN WITH FELT

Jane Yates

WINDMILL
BOOKS ™

Published in 2017 by **Windmill Books**, an Imprint of Rosen Publishing
29 East 21st Street, New York, NY 10010

Developed and produced for Rosen by BlueAppleWorks Inc.

Creative Director: Melissa McClellan
Managing Editor for BlueAppleWorks: Melissa McClellan
Designer: T.J. Choleva
Photo Research: Jane Reid
Editor: Kelly Spence
Craft Artisans: Jane Yates (p. 8, 10, 12, 14, 16, 20, 22, 24, 26, 28)

Cataloging-in-Publication Data

Names: Yates, Jane.
Title: Fun with felt / Jane Yates.
Description: New York : Windmill Books, 2017. | Series: Cool crafts for kids | Includes index.
Identifiers: ISBN 9781499482324 (pbk.) | ISBN 9781499482331 (library bound) |
  ISBN 9781508192817 (6 pack)
Subjects: LCSH: Felt work--Juvenile literature. | Felting--Juvenile literature.
Classification: LCC TT849.5 Y38 2017 | DDC 746'.0463--dc23

Manufactured in the United States of America
CPSIA Compliance Information: Batch #BW17PK:
For Further Information contact Rosen Publishing, New York, New York at 1-800-237-9932

CONTENTS

GETTING STARTED

Are you ready to have fun with felt? Felt is a material that is created by tightly packing and pressing together **fibers**. It can be made with natural fibers, like wool, or human-made fibers, like **acrylic**. Some kinds of felt are made by wetting lots of fibers and pressing them together so they dry as one piece of strong fabric. Others kinds are sewn together. Felt comes in a wide range of colors and **textures**. Most of the projects in this book can be made with either wool felt or acrylic felt.

You can purchase whatever you need at a craft store or dollar store. Organize your supplies in boxes or plastic bins. Then they are ready to use whenever you want to create felt projects.

RULER

SCISSORS

ACRYLIC FELT

WOOL FELT

FELT BALLS

Did You Know?

Many people still make felt. In Central Asia, people called **nomads** herd sheep. They use the wool from their flock to make felt. The fabric is used to make traditional rugs and clothing. It is also used to make tents called yurts. When the nomads travel, it is easy to roll up their tents to take with them.

CARDBOARD TOILET PAPER ROLLS

WHITE GLUE

YOU CAN ALSO USE FELT OR FABRIC GLUE.

PAPER

KEY RING

TAPESTRY YARN OR FINE YARN

PENCIL

YARN NEEDLE

A note about measurements

Measurements are given in US format with metric in parentheses. The metric conversion is rounded to make it easier to measure.

TECHNIQUES

Have fun while making your felt projects! Your projects do not have to look just like the ones in this book. Be creative and use your imagination. Working with felt is a great way to learn how to sew. Felt does not fray, so it does not need to be hemmed like regular fabric. You can practice your stitching on leftover pieces of felt. Use the following techniques to get started on your felt crafts.

THREADING A NEEDLE

Threading a needle takes practice. The following tips will help.

- Use a tapestry needle for felt work. It has a large opening for threading and a dull tip that will easily go through felt.

- Use a fine yarn or tapestry yarn.

- Fold a piece of yarn over, then push the fold through the opening. This is easier than using a single thread.

Put the yarn through the loop.

USING PATTERNS

- Patterns help you cut out exact shapes when sewing.

- Use tape or pins to attach the pattern to the felt before you start cutting.

- When cutting out a shape, cut around the shape first, then make smaller cuts.

- When cutting with scissors, move the piece of felt instead of the scissors.

- Make sure you keep your fingers out of the way while cutting. Ask an adult for help if needed.

Fold the yarn, then feed it through the loop.

Trace the pattern.

Cut the pattern out.

Attach the pattern to the felt.

Cut the felt along the pattern lines.

SEWING FELT

Use a whipstitch to sew two pieces of felt together along the sides.

- Thread a needle, then tie a knot at the other end.
- Place the needle and knotted thread in between the two pieces of felt. Push the needle through the top layer. Pull the thread through so the knot is hidden in between the layers.
- Loop the needle around the edges of the felt. Push the needle through both layers of felt to make your first full stitch.
- Angle the needle toward the spot where the next stitch will be.
- Continue stitching until finished.

Use a running stitch to sew one piece of felt on top of another piece.

- Thread a needle, then tie a knot at the other end.
- Place the needle and knotted thread underneath the two pieces of felt. Weave the thread in and out through both layers of felt.
- Continue stitching until finished.
- When you are done sewing, tie a knot on the back of the felt to hold the stitches in place.

BE PREPARED

- Read through the instructions. Make sure you have all the materials you need before you start.
- Clean up when you are finished making your project. Put away your materials for next time.

BE SAFE

- Ask for help when you need it.
- Ask for permission to borrow tools.
- Be careful when using scissors, pins, and needles.

FELT BALL NECKLACE

You'll Need:
- ✔ Felt balls
- ✔ Yarn
- ✔ Yarn needle
- ✔ Scissors

1 Make or purchase felt balls. If they do not have holes already, carefully push a yarn needle through the center of each ball.

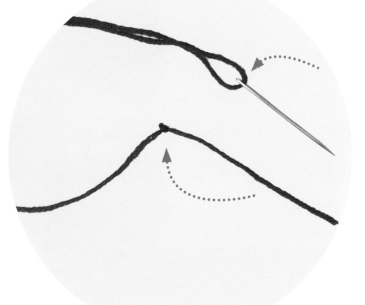

2 Measure out a piece of yarn. It needs to be a little bit longer than the final necklace length. Tie a knot at one end, then thread the other end through a yarn needle.

3 Make a second knot in the yarn about 2 inches (5 cm) from the knot at the end. Push the needle through the felt ball.

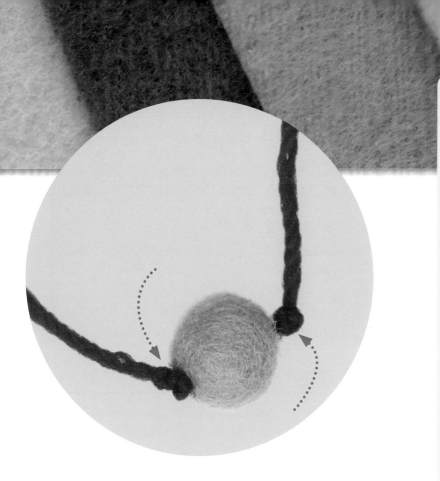

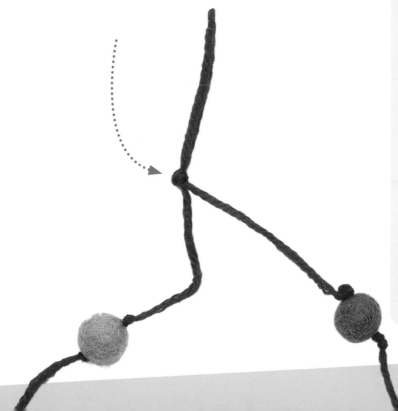

MAKE YOUR OWN FELT BALL

To make a felt ball, start with a small amount of 100 percent wool yarn. It will not work with a blend or acrylic. For a multicolored ball, use different colors of wool yarn.

1 Wind your yarn into a small ball. It will shrink, so it should be a little bigger than the final size you want the ball to be.

2 Soak the ball in warm, soapy water, then gently roll it between your hands for at least 5 minutes. Rinse out the soap, but do not squeeze the ball. Roll it in your hands a bit longer. Set it aside.

3 As the ball dries, it will harden as the fibers lock together.

4 Push the felt ball along the yarn to the knot. Tie another knot on the other side to hold it in place. Repeat Steps 3 and 4 until the necklace is full of balls.

5 Cut the yarn to remove the needle. Tie the two ends of yarn together.

STRIPED CONTAINER

You'll Need:

- ✔ Two cardboard toilet paper rolls
- ✔ Pencil
- ✔ Card stock or construction paper
- ✔ Scissors
- ✔ Masking tape
- ✔ Felt
- ✔ Glue
- ✔ Yarn

1 Trace around the end of the tube on card stock. Cut out the circle. Make a second circle and set it aside.

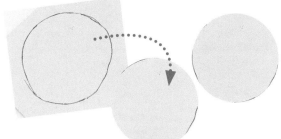

2 For the container, attach the circle to one end of the roll with masking tape. Crisscross strips of tape over the circle until it is covered. Wrap a long strip of tape around the tube to secure the ends.

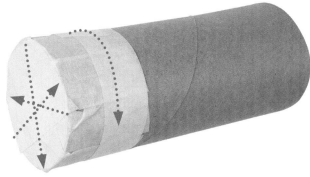

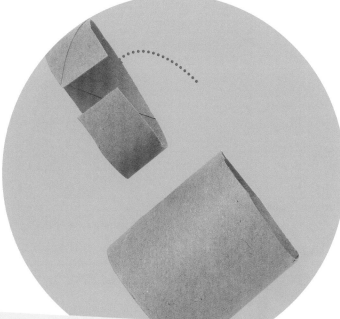

3 Cut one 2-inch (5 cm) piece and one 1-inch (2 cm) piece from the second roll. Make a slit in the smaller piece to form a C-shaped strip.

4 To make the lid, tape the second circle to the end of the shorter tube. Tape the smaller strip of cardboard halfway inside the lid as shown.

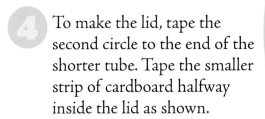

5 Measure and cut two pieces of felt that will wrap around each tube. Cut out a circle to cover the top of the lid. Cut some stripes to decorate the container.

6 Use the large pieces of felt to cover the rolls, then glue the stripes around the tube. Cut a small piece of yarn, then glue it around the edge of the lid to hide the seam.

Tip

When attaching felt, cover the entire piece with glue.

PENCIL TOPPERS

You'll Need:

- ✔ Felt
- ✔ Pencils
- ✔ Scissors
- ✔ Glue
- ✔ Googly eyes
- ✔ Rubber band

1 Trace one of the patterns on page 30 onto a piece of paper. Cut out the pattern. You can follow the same steps to make any of the pencil toppers.

2 Tape the patterns to a piece of felt. Cut out the pieces. Repeat this step so that you have a second head as well.

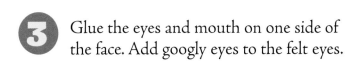

3 Glue the eyes and mouth on one side of the face. Add googly eyes to the felt eyes.

4 Cover the back of the head with glue. Place the pencil on top.

5 Place the other head piece on top, sandwiching the pencil in between the two pieces. Firmly press the two sides together. Wrap a rubber band around the end of the pencil to help hold the felt together.

Tip

When gluing two pieces of felt together, set the pieces under something heavy until the glue dries.

FUZZY FLOWERS

You'll Need:

- ✔ Felt
- ✔ Clear tape
- ✔ Scissors
- ✔ Buttons
- ✔ Glue or a needle and thread
- ✔ Green pipe cleaner

1 Trace the flower pattern pieces on page 31 onto a piece of paper. Cut out the pieces.

2 Tape each pattern piece to your felt pieces. Use the pattern as a guide to cut out the flower pieces.

3 Choose some colorful buttons that match the flowers.

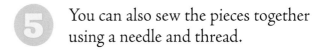

4 Glue the center piece onto the flower. Glue a button on top.

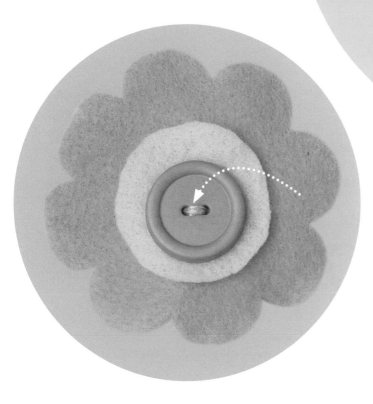

5 You can also sew the pieces together using a needle and thread.

6 If you are sewing the flowers together, add a stem by placing a green pipe cleaner behind the flower. Secure it with a stitch

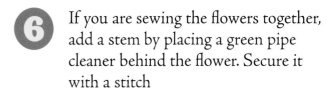

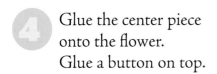

Tip

Turn your flower into a hair bow by gluing it onto a barrette.

FELT POUCH

You'll Need:

✔ Felt
✔ Scissors
✔ Marker
✔ Tape
✔ Cord or ribbon

1 Cut a 9-inch (23 cm) square of felt.

2 Trim the square into a circle.

3 Draw dots on the felt about ½ inch (1 cm) from the edge, and about ½ inch (1 cm) apart.

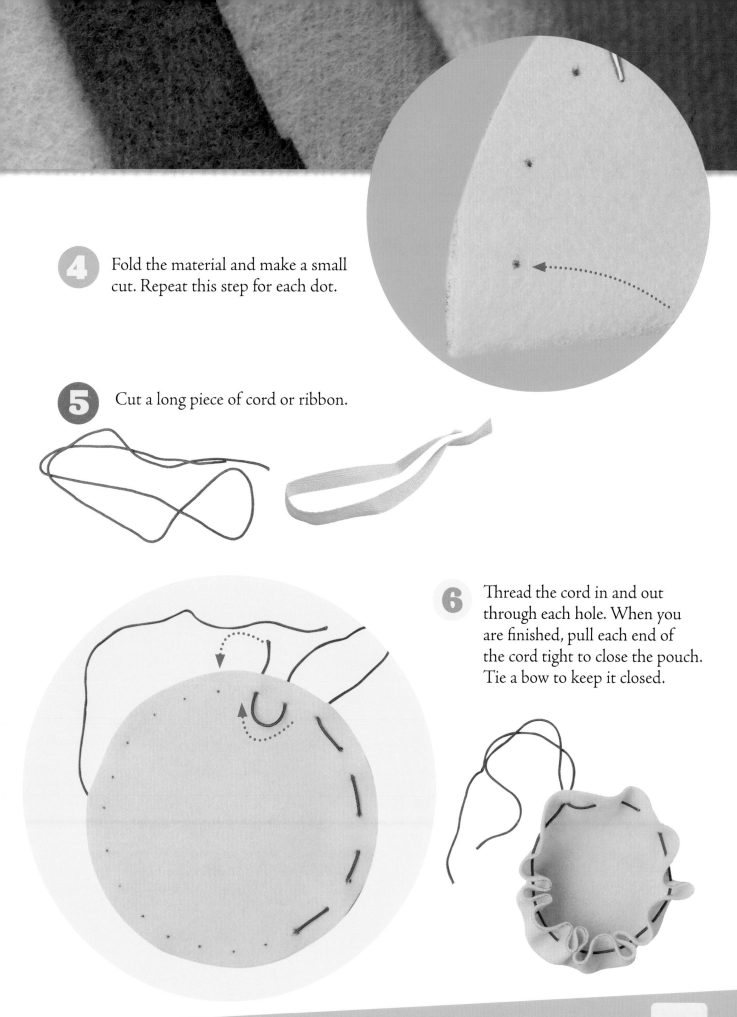

4 Fold the material and make a small cut. Repeat this step for each dot.

5 Cut a long piece of cord or ribbon.

6 Thread the cord in and out through each hole. When you are finished, pull each end of the cord tight to close the pouch. Tie a bow to keep it closed.

STUFFED MONSTER

You'll Need:

- ✔ Felt
- ✔ Paper
- ✔ Pencil
- ✔ Scissors
- ✔ Pins
- ✔ Needle
- ✔ Thread
- ✔ Stuffing or tissue paper

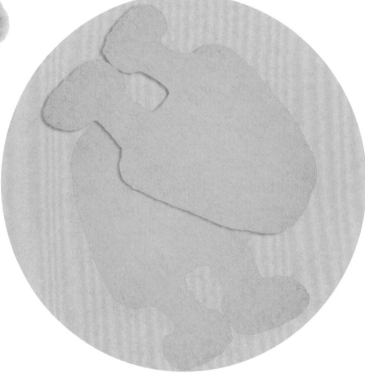

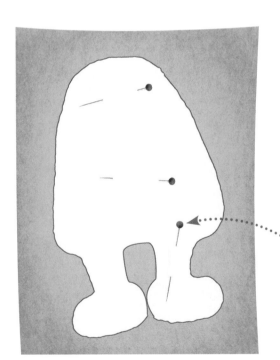

1 Trace the monster pattern on page 31. Cut out the pattern and pin it to the felt.

2 Cut out the pattern. Then pin it to a second piece of felt to make a second body piece.

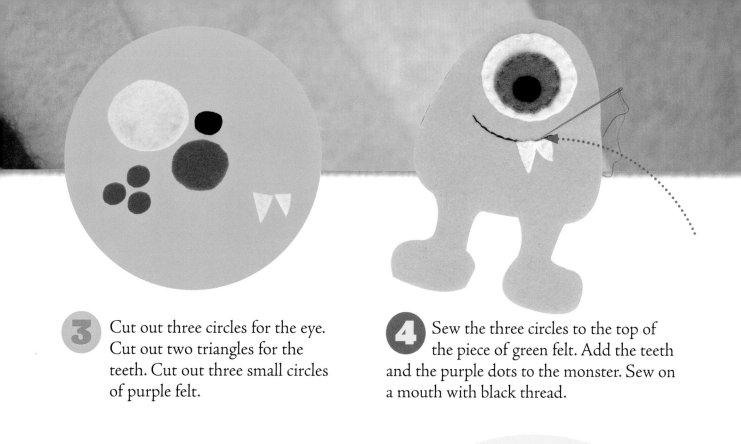

3 Cut out three circles for the eye. Cut out two triangles for the teeth. Cut out three small circles of purple felt.

4 Sew the three circles to the top of the piece of green felt. Add the teeth and the purple dots to the monster. Sew on a mouth with black thread.

5 Pin the two body pieces. Sew the two pieces together with a running stitch. Leave a small opening. Remove the pins.

6 Push stuffing through the small opening, then sew it shut.

Tip

Use thread that matches the color of the felt you are sewing.

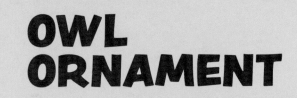

OWL ORNAMENT

You'll Need:

- ✔ Felt
- ✔ Paper
- ✔ Pencil
- ✔ Scissors
- ✔ Ribbon
- ✔ Glue
- ✔ Googly eyes
- ✔ Sequins

1 Trace the owl pattern pieces on page 31 onto a piece of paper. Cut out the pattern.

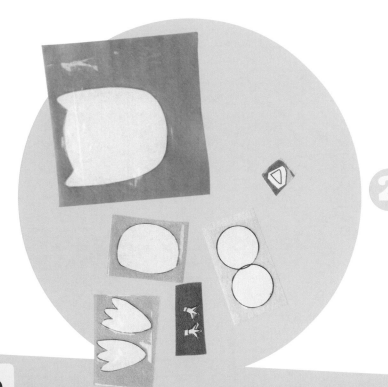

2 Tape the patterns to pieces of felt. Use different colors for each body part.

3 Cut out all the pieces.

4 Cut a 2-inch (5 cm) piece of ribbon. Glue the ends together to make a loop.

5 Glue googly eyes onto the owl's eye circles. Stick sequins onto the tummy circle.

6 Assemble the owl, gluing each piece in place. Glue the ribbon and legs to the back of the owl's body. Attach the loop to the back of the owl's head.

FINGER PUPPETS

You'll Need:

- ✔ Felt
- ✔ Paper
- ✔ Pencil
- ✔ Scissors
- ✔ Glue
- ✔ Stuffing
- ✔ Googly eyes

1 Trace the patterns on page 30 onto a piece of paper. Cut out the patterns. You can follow the same steps to make any of the finger puppets.

2 Fold a piece of felt in half. Tape the whale pattern to one side. Cut out the pattern, leaving a small section attached along the fold. You will now have two pieces of the same pattern joined at the fold.

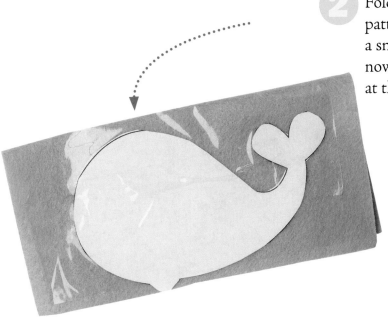

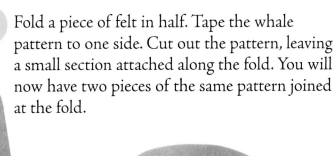

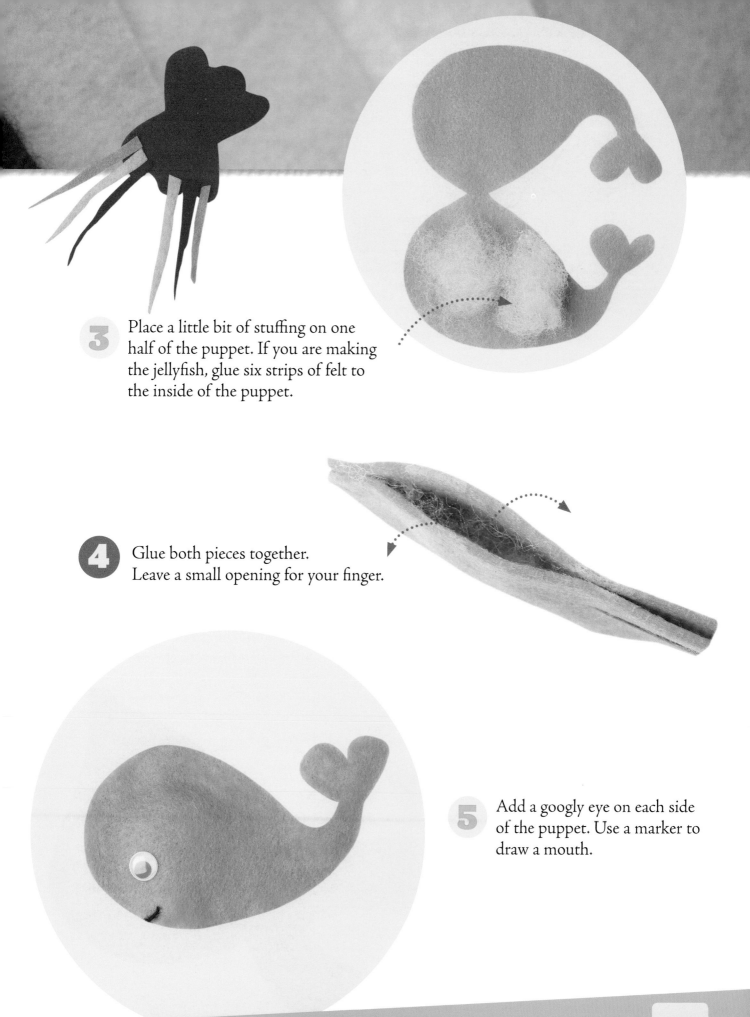

3 Place a little bit of stuffing on one half of the puppet. If you are making the jellyfish, glue six strips of felt to the inside of the puppet.

4 Glue both pieces together. Leave a small opening for your finger.

5 Add a googly eye on each side of the puppet. Use a marker to draw a mouth.

SUPERHERO MASK

You'll Need:

- ✔ Felt
- ✔ Pencil
- ✔ Paper
- ✔ Scissors
- ✔ Glue
- ✔ Elastic cord

1 Trace the mask pattern on page 31 onto a piece of paper. Cut out the pattern.

2 Tape the pattern to a piece of felt. Cut out the mask. Fold each eye in half to cut out the eyeholes.

3 Cut a piece of elastic cord long enough to reach around the back of your head. Cut two small holes in each side of the mask.

4 Knot each end of the elastic through the holes on the sides. Make sure the mask is not too tight.

5 Trace the lightning bolt pattern on page 31 onto a piece of paper. Cut out the pattern. Make two red lightning bolts and two yellow lightning bolts. Glue the red bolts above the eyeholes on the front of the mask. Trim the yellow bolts, then glue one below each eye to hide the elastic.

STAR KEYCHAIN

You'll Need:
- ✔ Felt
- ✔ Paper
- ✔ Pencil
- ✔ Scissors
- ✔ Glue
- ✔ Key ring

1 Trace the star pattern pieces on page 30 onto a piece of paper. Cut out the patterns.

2 Tape the patterns to felt, then cut out the pieces. Make two stars in each size.

3 Glue the smaller stars onto the larger pieces in layers as shown.

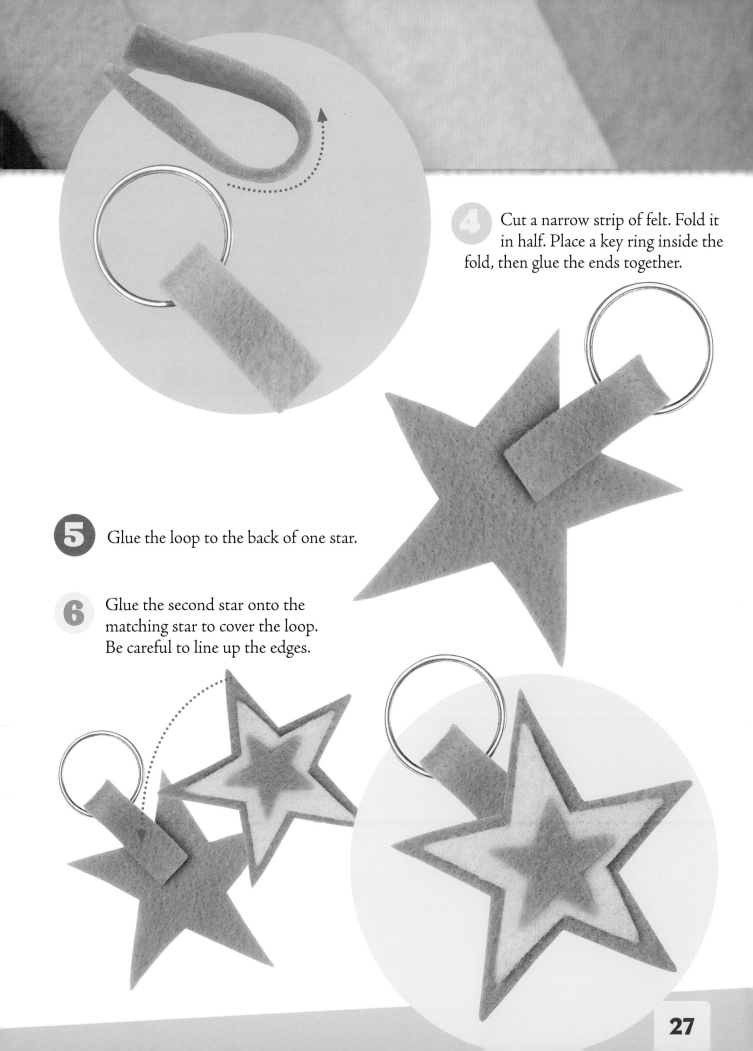

4 Cut a narrow strip of felt. Fold it in half. Place a key ring inside the fold, then glue the ends together.

5 Glue the loop to the back of one star.

6 Glue the second star onto the matching star to cover the loop. Be careful to line up the edges.

SUNGLASSES CASE

You'll Need:

- ✔ Felt
- ✔ Yarn needle
- ✔ Yarn
- ✔ Scissors
- ✔ Velcro dot

1 Place your sunglasses on a piece of felt. Fold it lengthwise, then cut along the sides around the glasses. Leave about a 1-inch (2 cm) border.

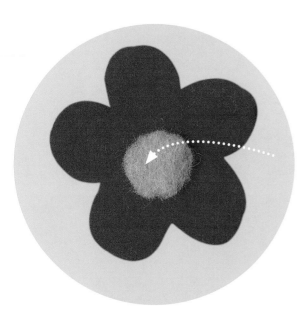

2 Cut a flower using the patterns on page 31. Glue the center to the flower.

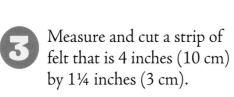

3 Measure and cut a strip of felt that is 4 inches (10 cm) by 1¼ inches (3 cm).

4 Sew or glue the flower onto the case. Sew the short piece to the long piece.

5 Use a whipstitch (see page 7) to sew the two sides of the case together.

6 For your case to close, you will need a Velcro dot. Place one half on the case and the other half on the flap. Make sure the two pieces line up when the flap is folded.

PATTERNS

Some pieces of the pattern are layered on top, so cut separate pattern pieces as indicated in the instructions.

STAR KEYCHAIN – PAGE 26

FINGER PUPPETS – PAGE 22

PENCIL TOPPERS – PAGE 12

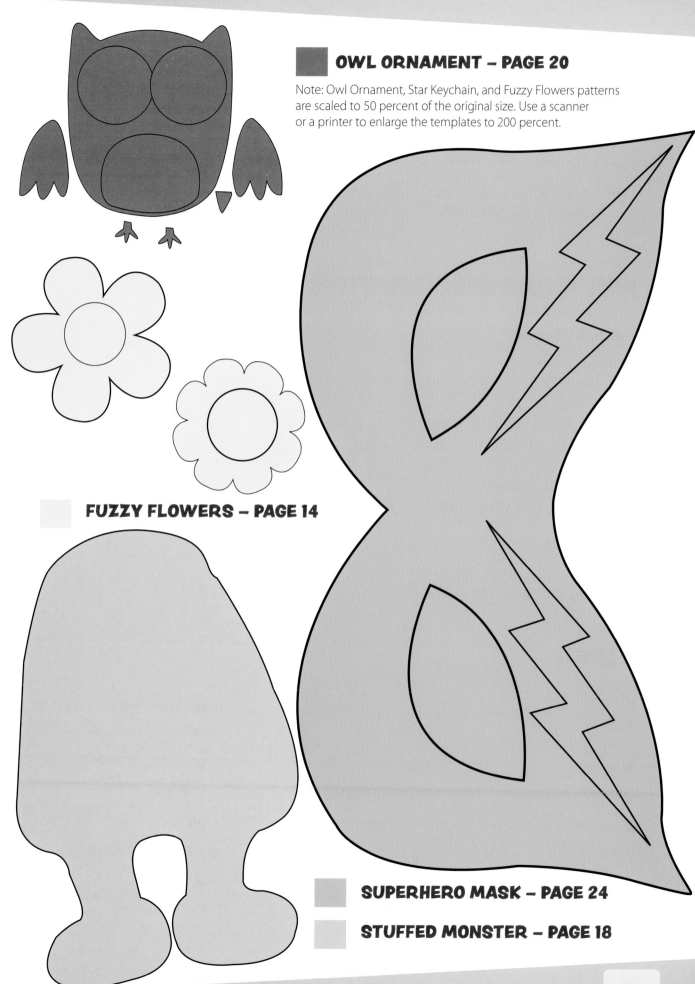

OWL ORNAMENT – PAGE 20

Note: Owl Ornament, Star Keychain, and Fuzzy Flowers patterns are scaled to 50 percent of the original size. Use a scanner or a printer to enlarge the templates to 200 percent.

FUZZY FLOWERS – PAGE 14

SUPERHERO MASK – PAGE 24

STUFFED MONSTER – PAGE 18

GLOSSARY

acrylic A type of human-made fiber used to make knit and woven cloth.

fibers Threads.

nomads People who wander from one place to another.

textures Ways that describe how a material feels.

FOR MORE INFORMATION

Further Reading

Bull, Jane. *Stitch-By-Stitch*.
New York: DK Publishing, 2012.

Carestio, Amanda. *Fa la la la Felt*.
New York: Lark Crafts, 2010.

Howard, Laura. *Super-cute Felt*.
New York: CICO Books, 2014.

WEBSITES

For web resources related to the subject of this book, go to:
www.windmillbooks.com/weblinks and select this book's title.

INDEX